Finding Out About
FIGHTING IN WORLD WAR I

Stephen Hoare

Batsford Academic and Educational *London*

Contents

Frontispiece:

A devastated landscape, Ypres, 1917. All that remains of a wood after prolonged artillery bombardment. Notice how duckboards are used to bridge the mud-filled shell craters.

To my Grandfather

© Stephen Hoare 1986
First published 1986

Typeset by Tek-Art Ltd, Kent
and printed in Great Britain by
R J Acford
Chichester, Sussex
for the publishers
Batsford Academic and Educational,
an imprint of B. T. Batsford Ltd,
4 Fitzhardinge Street
London W1H 0AH

ISBN 0 7134 5047 9

ACKNOWLEDGMENTS

I am grateful to all those who helped me research the material for this book. In particular, I wish to thank the staff of the Department of Documents at the Imperial War Museum for their unfailing helpfulness in sharing their specialist knowledge: Clive Hughes of the Department of Documents for recommending some particularly useful sources of information and for reading and commenting on my script; and Ms Sarah McConnell for her help with the picture research.

The following photographs are reproduced courtesy of the Imperial War Museum: frontispiece, pages 6 (below), 13 (above), 14, 15, 16, 17, 18, 19, 20, 21, 23, 26, 29, 30, 33 (below), 34, 36, 37, 38, 39, 42, 43. I am also grateful to Chris Overfield for photographic work.

The quotation from *Seven Pillars of Wisdom* on pages 22-23 is reprinted by kind permission of the Seven Pillars Trust and Jonathan Cape Ltd. The extract from *Testament of Youth* by Vera Brittain (page 43) is included with the permission of her literary executors and Victor Gollancz Ltd.

Lastly, I wish to thank my grandfather, Charles Hoare, who served in the Royal Engineers. He told me countless stories of his experiences in the First World War and awakened a lifelong interest in the subject.

Introduction

Each year in early November you will see people selling red paper poppies to collect money for injured ex-servicemen. These blood-red flowers grew wild on the battlefields of France and Belgium during the First World War. Today, the paper poppies are a reminder of the men who died there.

In the years from 1918 up to the Second World War many people believed there would never be another war. The Great War, as the 1914-18 war was then called, had been "a war to end wars".

This book looks at the Great War from the point of view of the men and women who served in the armed forces. The extracts from different documents will help you discover their reasons for fighting and how they carried on with their everyday lives. They will also make you want to find out other facts for yourselves.

What were the causes of the First World War? In the early years of this century there was an uneasy balance of power between the main countries of Europe. France and Russia had signed a pact in August 1891, each promising full military support if the other should be attacked by Germany. In 1904 and 1907 Anglo-French and Anglo-Russian ententes were signed. Germany was fast becoming a major economic and military power but she felt threatened by the dominant positions of Britain and France.

In eastern Europe Russia wanted to prevent the expansion of Germany's ally since 1879, the Austro-Hungarian Empire. Every major European country began to spend more and more money building bigger and better-equipped armies and navies. It needed only one small incident to upset the balance of power.

On 28 June 1914 Archduke Ferdinand of Austria was murdered by a Serbian nationalist in Sarajevo. As a result, the Austro-Hungarian Empire declared war on her tiny neighbour, Serbia. Russia came to Serbia's aid and ordered her army to prepare for war.

The leaders of Germany became anxious. Germany was Austria's ally. If Russia invaded Austria, then she might also attack Germany. Russia's ally, France, might seize her opportunity and attack Germany from the west. In 1905 the then chief of staff of the German army, Alfred Graf von Schlieffen, had devised a plan to deal with a two-pronged threat from France and Russia. If Russia ordered her army to mobilize, then the bulk of the German army would be sent immediately through neutral Belgium to attack France. Schlieffen's plan was to deliver a hammer blow to the French by cutting off the Channel ports and encircling Paris, forcing the French army to a quick surrender. By the time Russia could equip her army and send it into battle, German troops would be ready to defend their fatherland.

On 1 August 1914, Germany declared war on Russia. Two days later she declared war on France and sent her army marching through Belgium to attack France. As a result, Britain stepped in to defend Belgian neutrality and declared war on Germany. On 4 August Britain was at war.

When Britain and her allies eventually halted the advance of the German army in France and Belgium they dug trenches as a defence against attack. The Germans also dug lines of trenches and the two armies faced one another across a narrow strip of land — "no-man's-land". These lines of trenches were the famous Western Front. It is easy to forget that the years 1914 to 1918 also saw fighting in Russia, Greece, Turkey, Italy, Austria and Africa.

For one reason or another, all the major world powers became involved in the fighting, either to protect allies or to settle border disputes or to add to their colonial empires. Britain's allies included Japan, Italy, Russia and, from 1917, the United States.

The war was fought mainly on land. At sea

the British and the German navies were both powerful and evenly matched. After the indecisive battle of Jutland in 1916 neither side risked open battle again.

The First World War became a war of attrition – of each side trying to wear down the other in terms both of the amount of ammunition fired and of the huge numbers of soldiers killed. More than 700 million shells were fired on the Western Front alone during the war. France and Germany each lost around a million and a half men; Britain and her colonies lost one million and the USA 88,000. Russia lost more than all these numbers put together.

The beginning of 1918 saw the German army on the offensive. Everywhere the Allies had to fall back. But the German army, in leaving its prepared lines, was extending itself too far. Soon it was the turn of the Allies, supported by fresh, battle-ready American troops, to turn the tide of the German advance.

The German government not only faced military defeat; they also feared a revolution inside Germany similar to that which had occurred in Russia in 1917. On 9 November Germany's emperor, Kaiser Wilhelm II, abdicated. An armistice or ceasefire was signed between Germany and the Allies on 11 November 1918.

◁ A soldier and his sweetheart – two keepsakes of the Great War.

Useful Sources

1. PEOPLE

There are very few people alive today who fought in the First World War. Those who did are almost certainly in their nineties.

Your parents or grandparents may well have known and talked to older people who fought in the First World War. They may be able to tell you a few interesting stories about life at that time. If you have a portable cassette tape recorder, why not use it to record some of the things they tell you? People being interviewed will often "dry up" in front of a microphone, and so you will have to talk to a person for a little time, to bring back memories, before switching on your recorder. If the person being interviewed stops in the middle of what seems to be an interesting story, he or she may need a prompt. If you ask, "What happened then?" or "What did you think about . . . ?", your interviewee may well carry on and give a much more interesting and detailed account.

2. WRITTEN MATERIAL

a) *Memoirs and autobiographies* After the war a number of people who had witnessed events wrote a factual account of their experiences. Some of these were published. Ask your librarian if there are any autobiographies in the library by people who lived through the First World War. Several are listed on page 47. Other people's memoirs were not published but have often been donated to museums, such as the Imperial War Museum. This is where I found most of the material for this book.

Written material (documents) and tapes (sound archives) are kept in the Imperial War Museum's special collections and these may be visited on special request. The Museum's Education Department publishes its own book of facsimile documents for school use.

b) *Diaries* These too have often been donated to museums. Diaries and letters are less likely than memoirs written after the war to contain detailed information. This is because letters from servicemen were censored and it was against military regulations to keep detailed diaries. These regulations were made to prevent valuable information about troop movements and strengths from falling into enemy hands if a soldier were taken prisoner in a raid.

c) *Poetry* Poets often give a good idea of what the war meant to the individual. Men like Wilfred Owen, Siegfried Sassoon and Rupert Brooke paint a vivid picture of the emotions of servicemen when faced by death and destruction. What makes their poetry so vital is that it was written at the time the events described were taking place. The best-known anthology of war poetry, *Men Who March Away*, is listed on page 47.

d) *Songs* Your parents and teachers will almost certainly know the words to some of the songs of the First World War. If you have a music teacher, ask him or her to play the tunes for you. The most popular marching songs are "It's a Long Way to Tipperary" and "Pack Up Your Troubles in Your Old Kit Bag". There is a film and an LP record by EMI of Joan Littlewood's famous musical, *Oh What a Lovely War*. The musical contains many popular First World War songs.

e) *Newspapers and magazines* Newspapers and magazines of the period show the way the war was seen by people living at the time. But a word of warning: most of the articles you read will have been based on official government reports. Usually these present a more optimistic picture of the progress of the war than was normally the case at the time. Some museums and main libraries of big cities have kept archives of newspapers and magazines of the period. Of particular interest are *The Times, The Sketch, The Sphere, Illustrated London News* and *The War Illustrated*.

3. VISUAL MATERIAL

a) *Photographs* Most of the photographs you will see in books were official photographs taken by army photographers. Their job was to record the actions that were fought and to show life in the armed services. You will see few photographs of dead bodies and those you do see are usually German. It was thought to be unwise to publish photographs of the dead and wounded when the government was trying hard to recruit volunteers.

However, no photographer could hide the scenes of shattered, shell-torn landscapes and mud-filled trenches.

The Imperial War Museum has the biggest collection of official war photographs in the country and a pack of some of the most dramatic of these has been compiled for school use.

b) *Postcards* Antique fairs and junk shops are a good source for anyone wishing to buy postcards of the First World War. These are still very common and can be bought usually for under 50 pence. You will see that place-names on the cards have nearly always been deleted by the censor's blue pencil. Flanders was noted for its fine lace, and off-duty soldiers would often buy beautifully embroidered lace mounted on postcards to send back to girlfriends, wives and mothers in Britain. You can see an example of such a card on page 33.

c) *Mementoes* Not so long ago – perhaps as recently as the 1960s – many families still kept a display of photographs and war souvenirs. Nowadays you are more likely to find this sort of thing in junk shops or at flea markets. Soldiers made souvenirs out of highly polished brass shell and bullet cases – spent ammunition. Boxes, ash trays and all sorts of useful but ornamental objects were made by the troops in their spare moments. Often these are inscribed with the name of a famous battle or with the regimental crest.

4. PLACES TO VISIT

Those of you lucky enough to live in or near London will be able to visit the Imperial War Museum which, in addition to permanent displays of uniforms, weapons and equipment, often has temporary exhibitions which imaginatively reconstruct some aspect of the war with the aid of sound and photographs. The Museum's Education Department gives special talks for school children, where they are allowed to look at and handle exhibits not normally on show to the public. Film shows, too, are given.

Outside London, museums of local history and army regimental museums often have excellent displays on the First World War period.

Battlefield Tours Some schools organize visits to battlefields in Belgium and France. At places such as Ypres, Verdun and Beaumont Hamel on the Somme, whole sections of trenches and battlefield have been preserved. Much other evidence of the fighting is still left to see – large, water-filled craters, concrete pill-boxes and so on. The best guide to the battlefields of Europe is Rose Coombs' book, *Before Endeavours Fade*, published by Battle of Britain Prints International, 3 New Plaistow Road, London, E15.

This picture, entitled "How Guy Standish Won His V.C.", illustrated a story that appeared in a magazine in 1914. What view of warfare does it portray?

Volunteers

At the outbreak of war, Britain had a tiny regular army compared with Germany's. Lord Kitchener, Secretary of State for War, lost no time in building up Britain's army. He relied on volunteers.

Newspapers printed stories about the evil deeds done by the Germans. Most of these stories were either untrue or exaggerated. They were propaganda.

Kitchener's recruitment campaign was a great success. In the first month of war, 500,000 men volunteered. In the months that followed at least 100,000 men joined the armed forces every month.

By the end of 1915, however, the war was taking a turn for the worse. Victory was not in sight. In January 1916 Parliament passed a law making military service compulsory for all single men. In May conscription was extended to married men as well.

Many recruiting offices were simply booths set up in the street. The "office" here was set up in Trafalgar Square, London, in 1914. What purpose did the gramophone serve?

PATRIOTIC FERVOUR

William Quinton wrote an account of his First World War experiences, in 1929. The following extract describes how he joined the army in August 1914:

> **Every street corner was a recruiting office. Train loads of young men left the big towns and cities for the barracks and training centres. I was one of them. Just a drop in a vast ocean, but ready to do my bit with the rest. At Kempston barracks, Bedford I donned my suit of khaki and became a full-blown private in the Bedfordshire Regiment. With my new-found comrades, and the spirit of adventure bubbling over within me, I was ready to do my bit with the rest of them.**
> (Private William Quinton, 4th Battalion, Bedfordshire Regiment)

In 1914 the class system was more noticeable than it is today. Can you spot the differences between the recruits in this photograph? What kind of job do you think the man in the boater did?

UNDER-AGE SOLDIERS

Austin Heraty enlisted in the army at Newcastle-under-Lyme, Staffordshire on 6 September 1915. He served with the Royal Field Artillery for four years and fought at Ypres, the Somme, Vimy Ridge and Passchendaele. After the war he wrote about his experiences in an unpublished manuscript entitled *A Duration Man*.

A RECRUITING SONG

We've watched you play at cricket,
At every sort of game,
At football, golf and polo
You men have made your name.
But now your country calls you
To play your part in war
And no matter what befalls you
We shall love you all the more,
So come and join the forces like your
   fathers did before.

Oh we don't want to lose you,
But we think you ought to go,
For your King and your country
Both need you so.
We shall want you and miss you
But with all our might and main
We shall cheer you, thank you, kiss
   you,
When you come back again!
(Music and lyrics by Paul Rubens, 1914,
courtesy Chappell Music)

This music hall song was very popular at the beginning of the war. Would it have made you want to join up if you were a young man?

'Name please.'
'Austin J. Heraty, 15 Bailey Street, Newcastle.'
'Age?'
'18, sir.'
The sergeant looked up at me and said, 'Did you say 18, Mr Heraty?' I said, 'yes, sir.' There was a few moments of silence in the room and I stood there like a spare dinner . . . . I just turned around and began to walk out of the chamber, but before I could close the door after me, someone called out, 'come back here.' Of course, it was the listing sergeant. I walked back to the table and the sergeant said to me again, 'How old did you say you were, Mr Heraty?' (Still the penny had not dropped.) I said, '18, sir.' The sergeant looked up at me and said, 'I am very sorry Mr Heraty but I'll tell you what you can do. You can have a walk around the town, but if you come into this room again tonight, you must be 19 years of age.' (And then the penny did drop.) I was around the Town Hall in about 60 seconds flat, and was in the room before my pal Abe had got off the scales and went through a repeat of the previous question, name etc, age, '19 years of age, sir'. And I was in and signed and sealed and received the King's shilling. (Gunner Austin James Heraty, 80 Brigade, Royal Field Artillery)

Many even younger than Mr Heraty were allowed to join the armed forces and no questions were ever asked. What are your views? What was the King's shilling?

Preparing for Battle

In the early stages of the war, floods of men eagerly volunteered to join the army. The army, however, was not prepared for such vast numbers of new recruits. As regiments swelled in size with the new intake of men, extra battalions were formed. The men of these battalions were known as "Kitchener's army". Khaki uniforms were not available at first and so the men were kitted out in blue denim, as a temporary measure. Being sent overseas was a great adventure for most men. Few had ever travelled further than their nearest town or city.

TRAINING CAMP

Hiram Sturdy volunteered for the Royal Artillery in Caerphilly in September 1914. He arrived in France in March 1915 and served continuously on the Western Front. In this extract from his memoirs he describes the basic training he was given:

Preston Fulwood barracks was the first depot where with other thousands we hung around, waiting for our papers coming through before being fixed to a battery. That comes – the 8th Kitchener's Reserve Battery, and we start training. For a few weeks we train in our own civilian clothes, ranging from moleskins to the latest cut. Then we get our artillery uniform (blues) and one couldn't tell t'other from which, the moleskin man from the latest cut man.

Our sergeant (Fawcett) at first is in a policeman's uniform, and he too gets a rig out of khaki. Now we are soldiers.

Marching, running, jumping and jerks, we are soon in the pink of condition. We get gun drill, when we get guns, and learn how to 'take posts' and lay the gun with sights that I never saw afterwards. We were lined up before Christmas 1914 ready for overseas, but the order is cancelled. There is grumbling as some are afraid the show is going to be over before we get to it. (Gunner Hiram Sturdy, Royal Artillery)

Moleskin was the name of a thick material used to make workman's clothes. Why do you think the men were so pleased to get their army uniforms?

Why did many men believe that the war would be over by Christmas 1914?

THE ARRIVAL OF TROOPS IN FRANCE

Lieutenant Frank Bass of the 23rd Battalion, Middlesex Regiment, kept a diary throughout the war. On 14 September 1916 he described his arrival in France. (Despite the fact that keeping a diary was against regulations – it might fall into enemy hands if a soldier were captured – many officers kept detailed accounts of day-to-day events.)

Arrived at Boulogne at 4pm and lined up on the Boulevard. Marched to rest camp just outside, Cambs [Cambridgeshire Regiment] leading column. In tents for the night and paraded next morning at 9 a.m. to entrain for the base. French children very pretty and march along with us holding our hands. Some of them sell us chocolate, 'spearmint' and 'Dictionnaires' are also sold. Kiddies ask for cigarette 'peectoors' – only English they know. No two uniforms appear to be alike among the French. Can't tell whether soldier, sailor, gendarme, railway porter, taximan or postman. Everybody wears some sort of uniform and no two soldiers are dressed alike.

Do you know what cigarette pictures were? Do you know anyone who collects them?

Why do you think the people of Boulogne were so pleased to see British soldiers?

◁ *A line-up of new recruits in their khaki uniforms. Notice the bugler boy in the front row. How old do you think he is?*

BATTLE TRAINING

Etaples (the soldiers called it "Eat Apples") was the base camp from which troops were sent on to the front line. Lt Bass continued his diary:

**Etaples, Weds Sept 20th, 1916
Callousness of lectures shocks us. Marched to arena (sort of Greek amphitheatre holding about 1000) for lecture on bombs. Then break of ½ hour – mills bomb very important. Finished morning's work by passing through gas chamber in our helmets – phosgene and chlorine mixed. Played back to camp by bagpipes – very nice step.
Night ops at night. 6.30 to bull ring had short lecture and then to trenches. Didn't know what we were supposed to be doing or whereabouts we were. Strolled aimlessly about and one time found ourselves outside altogether. Never been on night ops which were any good – always a washout. Nobody knows what to do. Officers all swearing and given to confusion. Back to camp by midnight to bed.**

**Sunday Sept 24, 1916
Reveille at 5.30 again and parade to bull ring. Not much work though for which we are very thankful. Lectures all morning, all our instructors giving us their experiences at the front. All these men seem particularly callous and talk of killing as nothing at all. 'Remember boys', one of them said, 'every prisoner means a day's rations gone.'**

What is Lt Bass's chief impression of warfare? Do you think the training he gets will prepare him for conditions in the trenches? What other information would a soldier need before he went into battle?

"Bull" is a slang word for routine discipline. What do you think the "bull ring" is and what do soldiers do there?

The Infantry

The British army of the First World War contained 75 infantry regiments, including 5 guards regiments. These were the foot soldiers – the men who bore the brunt of the fighting.

Although the infantry made up just under half the fighting strength of the British army, they suffered a far greater casualty rate than any other branch. Out of a total of 764,172 officers and men killed, 588,526 belonged to infantry regiments – 77% of the total.

The infantry regiments were organized in battalions of roughly 1000 men. Regiments of infantry were conscripted from counties or cities. The men who joined them therefore shared a strong sense of local tradition. The largest regiments were those drawn from the major cities. The Royal Fusiliers drew its men entirely from London and had 49 battalions, while the Connaught Rangers from Ireland had only 6 battalions.

Rolls of Honour like this appeared each week in magazines and newspapers and gave a list of officers killed. No mention was made of the thousands of ordinary soldiers killed.

THE ROLL OF HONOUR

Pro patria mori

A housewife – pronounced "hussif" – was a pack containing needles and thread for making emergency repairs to a soldier's uniform. What purpose do you think each of the other items served?

AN INFANTRY ATTACK

Sergeant George Harbottle was lucky to survive the attack on St Julien in the Ypres salient on 26 April 1915. In 1980 he wrote and published a book about his active service, called *A Civilian Soldier 1914-1919*. In 1985, seventy years after his lucky escape, 92-year-old George Harbottle is still working as a coal importer in his native city of Newcastle.

All we knew was that we had to 'fall in' with full equipment, i.e. full marching order with pack on our back containing great coat and all our spare

possessions. Add to this ammunition pouches, rifle, haversack and entrenching tool, plus two extra bandoliers of ammunition just served out to us, it is obvious we were well weighted down.

Anyway we moved off as a battalion somewhere about 2.00 pm. shaking out to columns of companies, then into columns of platoons all just as we had been trained to do in mock fights at home . . . . Consequently we were suddenly faced with an impenetrable line of barbed wire about four yards in depth, which was our own GHQ reserve line. There were some gaps to get through but very few and far between . . . .

By good fortune 'A' company was leading and my section was one of the first through the gap as we had arrived just beside one. We were then in extended order in true drill book fashion and advanced in short sharp rushes under whistle command. Our packs were a terrible encumbrance and so out came jack knives and we just cut the straps of each other's packs and left them behind. Those who did survive, lived for the next few months sans [without] greatcoat or any spare clothing. We had a lot of casualties coming down that slope, from both shrapnel and machine gun fire, but the main slaughter was at the gaps getting through the wire . . . . The casualties on that St. Julien attack were 14 officers and 604 other ranks. Seven of the 14 officers were killed. (Sergeant George Harbottle, 6th Battalion, Northumberland Fusiliers)

ON THE MARCH

In January 1916 the division with which Hiram Sturdy was serving was sent from Armentières to the Loos front. This entailed a four-day march. At night the men slept wherever they could find shelter – usually in barns but on one occasion in the corner of a school playground. Can you imagine sleeping outside in the coldest month of the year?

On our march there are times when it is really grand. One of these occasions was on a beautiful, healthy frosty morning. After we have got a nice natural heat into the body we are on the outskirts of a forest, and we hear the strains of a brass band in a marching tune. As we draw closer we see the battalions of infantry coming in different directions but all heading south. One of the times when one feels proud, and wants to shout out and sing at the joy of life. A division on the move was a great sight and enjoyed by most until one's feet got a bit sore and kit a bit heavy, then the glamour gradually faded but these things were forgotten soon, if at the end of the day, there was a good rest or a decent place to sleep, but neither of these things were often at the end of the road. (Memoirs of Gunner Hiram Sturdy, Royal Artillery)

Can you explain why the men seemed to enjoy marching? What other moments of a soldier's life might he find enjoyable?

How does Sergeant Harbottle survive the attack? What mistakes do you think were made in planning the attack?

Horses

REQUISITIONING HORSES

In Britain, horses were requisitioned for army service. Their owners were forced to sell them to the government. At that time, most commercial transport was horse-drawn.

Later, half a dozen or so parties each in charge of a subaltern paraded and left in different directions to requisition horses, and from then onwards for the next few days the said parties returned leading two horses each of which were turned loose into one of the largest fields I have ever seen to await selection and allocation until each man of the 300 was properly mounted. One of the parties went as far afield as Streatham (of all places) and all parties searched diligently among riding schools, bus stables, big commercial depots and even valuable hunters were not spared. Inevitably when the concentration of horse flesh was inspected, small and ill-nourished animals were found and quietly put aside for resale to anyone who wanted them. The officers in charge were provided with government warrants to pay for the horses and the average price paid was about £40, too much for a horse or pony from a greengrocer's cart and too little for a hunter, but then the country was at war and horses must be found. (Memoirs of Private A.S. Benbow, West Kent Yeomanry)

What are your views about requisitioning? If the government decided to requisition your home in a national emergency how would you react? Where would you look for horses nowadays? Could you expect to find 300 horses in just a few days?

The British army in 1914 was ill-equipped for war. Most of their weapons, equipment and transport were out of date and in short supply. Horses still had an important part to play in wartime.

In 1914 the most prestigious units of the British army were the cavalry regiments — dragoons, lancers and hussars who rode into battle with sword or lance just as they had done in the wars against Napoleon a century earlier.

Teams of horses, ponies or even mules were used to pull the heavy field guns on the battlefield, while horse-drawn limbers or carts were used to transport supplies up to the front line.

Many horses were killed in action. By 1917 the army had 869,931 horses on active service.

A CAVALRY CHARGE

The cavalry charge described in this report took place at the battle of Mons when the tiny British Expeditionary Force under the command of Field Marshal Sir John French were fighting a rearguard action. Three hundred thoroughbred horses lost their lives in this charge.

The 9th Lancers seem to have repeated, under almost identical conditions, the famous Charge of the Light Brigade at Balaclava. Under a hail of lead they rode at a battery of eleven German guns which, posted inside a wood, were causing terrible loss amongst our infantry. Nothing could stop the infuriated horses and men. They reached the battery, cut down all the gunners, and put the guns out of action. The Duke of Westminster and Captain Grenfell took prominent parts in this heroic operation. (*The War Illustrated*, 12 September 1914)

A horse flounders in the mud while the water cart it is pulling has sunk to its axle.

HORSES ARE KILLED

The Pitiable Martyrdom of Man's Faithful Friend

Perhaps the most pitiable aspect of this war is the destruction in tens of thousands of man's faithful friend – the horse. Innocent, trustful, nervous, it is forced to assist its master in fighting his battles. A troop horse is believed to enjoy the wild delirium of a charge almost as highly as the rider upon its back, but the pained accusing look that enters its eyes when it is wounded is heart-searching to see. Horses maimed by shell fire are put out of their pain as speedily as possible, the Army Veterinary Corps and its helpers carrying an instrument for the painless despatch of all horses that are injured beyond hope of recovery.

Destruction of horses – artist's impression of the rearguard battle fought by men of the Royal Horse Artillery during the retreat from Mons, 1914. Do you know what ceremonial duty the Royal Horse Artillery performs today?

A great sympathy exists between cavalrymen and their chargers, and there have been many instances of horsemen, with tears in their eyes, giving their wounded animals a fond caress, and then putting them out of their agony. (*The War Illustrated*, 3 October 1914)

Do you agree that the wholesale destruction of horses was "the most pitiable aspect" of the war?

Some people seem to feel more for animals than for human beings. If a horse and its rider were killed in battle, which one would you feel the most pity for?

Would you describe the cavalry charge as "heroic"? Do you think the cavalry had a useful part to play in war?

Women at War

In 1914 the Women's Suffrage movement was at its height. Women were campaigning for the right to vote in Parliamentary elections. When war was declared, many women wanted to volunteer for national service as men were able to. But there was little opportunity for them.

Qualified nurses could volunteer for the army. Untrained women could join the British Red Cross as trainee nurses, cooks or ambulance drivers. These Red Cross volunteers were known as VADs because they formed a Voluntary Aid Detachment. As VADs were not usually paid, only women from well-off, middle-class homes could afford to join.

In 1915 the British army suffered heavy losses on the Western Front. The Government realized that if women were enlisted in the army as clerks, quartermasters and drivers, more men could be released for fighting. On 20 February 1916 the Women's Auxiliary Army Corps was formed.

WOMEN URGENTLY WANTED *for the* **W·A·A·C**
WOMEN'S ARMY AUXILIARY CORPS
WORK AT HOME AND ABROAD WITH THE FORCES
COOKS CLERKS WAITRESSES DRIVER-MECHANICS
ALL KINDS *of* DOMESTIC WORKERS & WOMEN *in* MANY OTHER CAPACITIES TO TAKE THE PLACE OF MEN
GOOD WAGES · QUARTERS UNIFORM · RATIONS
FOR ALL INFORMATION & ADVICE APPLY AT NEAREST EMPLOYMENT EXCHANGE
THE ADDRESS CAN BE OBTAINED AT ANY POST OFFICE

VADs

Lorna Neill was 22 when she joined the VADs as an ambulance driver. In the following extract from her memoirs, written during the 1960s, she describes her reception at the base camp in France.

Etaples 1917

Shortly we found ourselves in a large wooden hut with long tables along the sides and a large black stove at one end. Round this were sitting a most alarming collection of young or youngish women. They were wearing undress uniform consisting of long black boots, navy skirts which would look very long today, and sweaters. Beside each driver was a greatcoat, gloves and a navy peaked cap. They were waiting for the call from the officer, 'Trains coming in', which I got to know so well. Of course, we were in uniform ourselves ... wearing smart skirts with black ties under our navy uniform jackets. But although we were slightly the worse for wear after our journey, we were still shiny and had 'new boy' written all over us. I say 'new boy' because the whole thing was run on the lines of a tough boys' public school. These drivers looked on us with what appeared to be disdain. But we were given a good meal and went to bed. What's more, we slept.

What gave Lorna Neill the impression that the unit she joined was run like a "tough boys' public school"? What sort of behaviour would you have expected to find in a public school in those days?

◁ *This poster advertises the newly-formed WAAC. Does it tell you why women were needed by the army?*

If VADs were to set an example to others, they had to follow the code of conduct shown here. Why would it have been difficult to have put these good intentions into practice? ▷

AMBULANCE DRIVING

That night was as bad as I had ever anticipated. The first call came as usual about 9.00 pm and I dashed out amongst the others on to the lines. I did not have much difficulty in finding my bus as I had walked round and round it in daytime with the day duty driver who had been helpful. She explained that newcomers always got the oldest cars and pointed out the quirks of our mutual bus. She was quite new herself and had not yet been on night duty. She told me that the worst thing about No. 896 was a slipping clutch.

That night was bad. In spite of the efforts of my opposite number, 896 was very slow in starting and I was the last out of the lines, but just able to make out the car ahead and follow it. I got to a wide entrance – plenty of room – and saw Chambers standing. She shouted out a number to me and I went on. There standing and looking ominous and mysterious with dim lights in the coaches whose doors were now open, stood the long hospital train.

. . . I found out later that not only did the newcomer get the worst car but the last car at the train got the worst cases. This was because they needed more careful handling from the nurses on the train and probably four bearers on the stretcher. When the other cars were loaded there was more time to get this extra help. That night I only had one case, a man with a bad head wound and a wound in his stomach. 'Take care of him, driver' the nurse called to me as the men pushed the stretcher into the ambulance. (Lorna Neill, VAD)

No. 6773

This paper is to be considered by each V.A.D. member as confidential and to be kept in her Pocket Book.

You are being sent to work for the Red Cross. You have to perform a task which will need your courage, your energy, your patience, your humility, your determination to overcome all difficulties.

Remember that the honour of the V.A.D. organisation depends on your individual conduct.

It will be your duty not only to set an example of discipline and perfect steadiness of character, but also to maintain the most courteous relations with those whom you are helping in this great struggle.

Be invariably courteous, considerate, unselfish and kind.

Remember that whatever duty you undertake, you must carry it out faithfully, loyally, and to the best of your ability.

Rules and regulations are necessary in whatever formation you join. Comply with them without grumble or criticism and try to believe that there is reason at the back of them though at the time you may not understand the necessity.

Sacrifices may be asked of you.

Give generously and whole-heartedly, grudging nothing, but remembering that you are giving because your Country needs your help.

If you see others in better circumstances than yourself, be patient and think of the men who are fighting amid discomfort and who are often in great pain.

Those of you who are paid can give to the Red Cross Society which is your Mother and which needs more and more money to carry on its great work.

Those of you who are not paid are giving their best to their Mother Society and thus to the Sick and Wounded.

Let our mottoes be—" Willing to do anything " and " The People gave gladly."

If we live up to these, the V.A.D. members will come out of this world-war triumphant.

Do your duty loyally.
Fear God.
Honour the King.
KATHARINE FURSE,
Commandant-in-Chief, B.R.C.S. Women's V.A.D.s.

Car maintenance – a VAD ambulance driver looks under the bonnet. Girls were expected to service and repair their own vehicles.

At the time of the First World War, women were campaigning for equal rights. Can you see why women might have enjoyed life as VADs?

Would the life of a VAD appeal to a modern-day girl?

The War at Sea

As an island, Britain saw the importance of a large, well-equipped navy even before war started. At the outbreak of war, Britain had 580 fighting ships against the German navy's 327. The numbers of battleships and battle cruisers were closely matched on both sides.

All the large naval actions of the war took place in the first two years and Britain scored some notable successes in the battles of the Falklands and the Dogger Bank. When the British and German battle fleets met at Jutland, off the coast of Denmark, the result was stalemate. In the battle of Jutland, the British lost more ships than the Germans – three battle cruisers, three cruisers and eight destroyers – but the enemy fled to the safety of her own ports. German naval chiefs realized that their fleet was not strong enough to win a decisive naval battle. From then on they concentrated on building submarines to attack British merchant ships and cut off Britain's supplies of imported food and raw materials. To beat this menace, merchant ships were forced to travel in large formations called convoys.

A STOKER'S TALE

The battle of Heligoland Bight, off the coast of Germany, took place on 28 August 1914. Joseph Leach, a stoker in the engine room of the destroyer HMS *Hind*, recorded his impressions of that day.

Full speed ahead! More steam!

The telegraph clanged. We opened everything wide, and are kept very busy in the maintaining of two hundred and twenty five pounds of steam per square inch in the boilers as it is utilised by the engines for the tactics required from the bridge. We are in action! Our guns belch forth death and destruction above our heads and the ship reels drunkenly under the violent concussions.

The boiler room in a naval action must be the nearest approach to Hell on this planet. White hot furnaces! The boilers vibrating with their terrific high pressure. If a shell put the forced draught fans out of action, we would be charred to cinders by liquid flame in the back flash that would surely follow if the air pressure was cut off. And if a shell wrecked the boilers we would be boiled.

We must not let our imagination run riot down here but it is hard to keep one's thoughts from straying to these things. This kind of fighting demands the purest form of courage. A man has to exercise perfect mastery over his emotions, carrying out his duties in a

◁ *A First World War battle cruiser. In what ways have modern warships changed in appearance? What was the importance of the observation platforms on the masts?*

The navy's secret weapon, HMS Furious. *No photograph of this aircraft carrier was ever allowed to be published during the war.*

A GUN BATTLE

As each gun was fired a spurt of flame shot out of the muzzle, rapidly followed, so it seemed, by a handful of smoke which would rise in stately fashion above our ships, drifting ring-shaped over them for all the world like a leisurely smoker blowing rings from his cigar. And then about fifteen seconds after the flash – and what an age this fifteen seconds seemed! – a white splash of water would shoot up near the distant enemy.

This splash anxiously awaited by the gunnery control officers of the firing ship, gave the means of judging whether the shot fell short of, or beyond, the enemy. Based on this would come a rapid decision by the control officer; an order passed to the guns; the gun sights altered; the guns themselves relaid on the distant smoke smudge; an order to fire passed to all gun layers – and another spurt of flame. Then smoke issued from the cocked up muzzles, as two-thirds of a ton of metal searched hungrily for a victim . . .

One does not see that 'immense flash followed by an explosion rending the great ship in twain', which some imaginative mind has pictured, for a shell striking a ship is unobtrusive in its deadliness until it becomes the cause of a fire, or mayhap an explosion. In fact a hit is usually less noticeable than a miss.

Perhaps the most impressive feature of a modern naval action is the cold blooded devilry with which shots fall on and around a target so far away, searching out their victim with an apparent unconcern and simplicity, which is so much at variance with the deadly effect if they hit. (From an article entitled "I saw Beatty Triumph", by an officer on HMS *Aurora*, published in *I Was There*, Amalgamated Press, 1935)

mechanical manner. I glance at my two companions. I know they are thinking the same things as I am. We laugh! Each tries to convey to the other that we don't care a damn. But it is a pretence and a poor one to boot. (From an article entitled "Heligoland: A Stoker's Saga", published in *I Was There*, Amalgamated Press, 1935)

Do you agree that a stoker's job demands the most courage in a battle? Which other crew members might also claim that their job requires the "purest form of courage"?

In this article, the officer is describing the Battle of the Dogger Bank (24 January 1915), in which the German battle cruiser, *Blücher*, was sunk. If naval warfare from the time of the First World War was considered to be "cold blooded devilry", what aspects of modern warfare could be described in the same terms?

War in the Air

At the outbreak of the First World War, flying was in its infancy. The army and the navy both made use of planes for observation and had separate air services – the Royal Flying Corps and the Royal Naval Air Service. At the end of the war these combined to form the Royal Air Force.

OBSERVATION

Planes were used to spot enemy positions and look for troop movements. The pilot usually carried an observer in his plane, who marked the enemy's position on a map or took photographs, for use in planning a ground attack.

The following extract is from the memoirs of Major W.R. Read of the RFC. It dates from the very beginning of the war when he was a lieutenant.

Observers were posted to each flight and we had two – Capt Jackson and Capt Evans .... One day after our reconnaissance over Mons and Charleroi, Jackson spotted a German Taube machine. I had also seen him but we had done our job and I did not want a fight. Jackson, however, was always bloodthirsty and the following conversation ensued.

Jackson 'Look old boy.' Me 'Yes, I know.' Jackson 'I think we ought to go for him old boy.' Me 'Better get home with your report.' J.'I think we ought to go for him old boy.' Me 'All right.' I changed course for him and as we passed the Taube, Jackson got in two shots with the rifle. I suppose they did

Pilot's log book. Notice how often this fighter plane is used for observation. What other purposes does it serve?

Before aircraft carriers were developed, planes were ▷ launched, like the Sopwith Strutter in this photograph, from the gun platforms of battle cruisers. When a mission was completed, the pilot had to ditch his plane in the sea and wait to be rescued.

too. We turned and passed them again, with no obvious result. This happened three or four times. Then J. said 'Have you got a revolver old boy? Ammunition all gone.' I, feeling rather sick of the proceedings said 'Yes. No ammunition.' J. 'Give it me old boy and this time fly past him as closely as you can.' I carried out the instructions and to my amazement as we got opposite the Taube, Jackson, with my army issue revolver grasped by the barrel, threw it at the Taube's propeller. Of course it missed and then honour being satisfied, we flew home.

Do you think Captain Jackson was taking the war seriously? Find out what developments took place in aerial warfare during the First World War.

SHOOTING DOWN A ZEPPELIN

From 1915-16 Germany's big Zeppelin airships made frequent bombing raids on English towns and cities. For the first time in British history war was brought to the doorsteps of the civilian population.

In 1916 Flight Lieutenant Bernard Smart of the RNAS became a national hero for shooting down Zeppelin L23 over the North Sea. He wrote the following letter to a relative soon after the event described.

HMS Yarmouth   **21.8.1917**

I was now at 7000 feet and the Zep a thousand feet below, at an angle of 45 degrees, and I was still heading straight for her stern. I pushed forward the control stick and dived. The speed indicator went with a rush up to 150 mph and I was aiming to cut under the Zep a few yards astern of her.

The roar of the engine had increased to a shrill scream while the wires were whistling and screeching in an awful way.

I completely lost my head – the earth, sky and sea vanished and for the moment my universe consisted of that great round silvery object, myself and space.

Everything then happened automatically. 250 yards astern and same height as Zep, I flattened out slightly and pulled the lever which works the machine gun. I had misjudged the angle at which this was mounted and saw the white streaks of incendiary bullets going too high.

In a flash I had nosed down again, and rammed down the machine gun operating lever again and held it there. The gun spat out and although the flame was wobbling on account of the extreme sensitiveness of the controls due to the enormous speed, I had just time to see about half a dozen actually enter the blunt end of the Zep and a spurt of flame, before my soul froze with the thought that in my eagerness to aim the gun I had waited too long and couldn't avoid a collision. (Flight Lieutenant Bernard Smart, DSO, Croix de Guerre, Royal Naval Air Service)

Bernard Smart was one of the "air aces" of the First World War. Would he have become a national hero today for shooting down an enemy airship?

What can you find out about other air aces of the First World War?

Gallipoli

In October 1914 Turkey entered the war as an ally of Germany and her army surged over the border to attack Russia. Turkey also held the narrow straits of the Bosphorus and cut Russia's sea route to the west, effectively isolating her from her allies, Britain and France. Russia, hard pressed by Germany to the west, asked for British assistance. Winston Churchill, then First Lord of the Admiralty, put forward a plan for a seaborne attack at Gallipoli, on Turkey's Aegean coast.

After a naval bombardment in the early part of 1915 a task force was sent to land troops. The first landings took place on 25 April. Australian and New Zealand troops (ANZACS) were used as part of the first attack. They gave their name to the place where they landed – Anzac Cove.

The Gallipoli campaign was mismanaged from the start, despite some hard-won victories against the Turks. Troops suffered appalling casualties for little or no tactical gain. With the sea at their backs and with problems of keeping supplies of ammunition moving up to the front line, the British were forced to withdraw. The evacuation of Gallipoli fortunately went much more smoothly than the first landings and by 8 January 1916 all troops had been moved to safety.

ANZACs charge into battle.

The extracts in this section come from articles in a magazine called *I Was There* (Amalgamated Press, 1935).

THE LANDING AT ANZAC COVE

We were about thirty yards away when the pinnace cast off. No sooner were the oars in position, than – bang! From the right came the shrapnel. The Turks on the cliff and in the trenches were pouring forth a murderous fire from rifle and machine gun. The range was point blank, and how they missed any of us is hard to say.

No orders were given – or wanted – then. Every man not disabled at once jumped overboard. I handed my rifle to a sailor to hold and went over into the water up to my armpits. The poor fellow was handing my rifle back to me when a shrapnel shell burst just overhead and killed him. (From an article entitled "Through Death Valley With the Anzacs" by Private Fred Fox, Australian Imperial Force)

A pinnace was a small steam-powered launch used to tow groups of rowing boats towards the shore. In what ways were the landing craft used in the Second World War an improvement?

FIGHTING A LOSING BATTLE

In his article entitled "Men into Beasts" Digger Craven of the Australian Imperial Force described the aftermath of the battles at Anzac Cove from 28-30 June 1915. In the first attack, the Australian infantry gained 1000 yards of ground. The Turks mustered an army of 30,000 men to drive them back into the sea. In spite of overwhelming odds the Australians held on and at the end of the day the Turks withdrew, having suffered nearly 8000 casualties.

> **Dead lay around the trenches and between the lines, friend and foe rotting in the sun. The incessant tunneling of both sides had drawn us closer together. In some parts we were less than eighty yards from each other. That meant a never ending watch, never to relax for a second. Sentry duty at these points was a ghastly nerve strain, a perpetual agony with every faculty on edge, so that men had to be relieved at very short intervals.**
>
> **And as the summer advanced the conditions grew worse and worse. Dysentery took a very heavy toll. Water was scarce and strictly rationed. There were increasing cases of jaundice. There were septic sores, unclean ulcers, rat bites that nothing seemed to heal, and lice beyond all human control. The trenches were always full of black flies.**
>
> **We cursed the sun and the flies and the lice as enemies more terrible than the Turks.**

The soldier on the left is peering into a periscope ▷ while on the right a soldier is looking through a system of mirrors to fire a rifle mounted on a wooden framework. Why was this strange equipment used?

TURKISH SNIPERS

At Gallipoli sailors were issued with rifles and fought on land. As the photograph shows, they wore khaki uniforms and naval hats. A.P. Herbert, Royal Naval Division, described conditions:

> **So the sniping was terrible. In that first week we lost twelve men each day; they fell without a sound in the early morning as they stood up from their cooking at the brazier, fell shot through the head, and lay snoring horribly in the dust; they were sniped as they came up the communication trench with water, or carelessly raised their heads to look back at the ships in the bay; and in the night there were sudden screams where a sentry had moved his head too often against the moon. If a periscope were raised, however furtively, it was shivered in an instant; if a man peered over himself, he was dead.** (From an article entitled "Gallipoli: Snipers' Paradise and Soldiers' Hell")

From the descriptions of Digger Craven and A.P. Herbert, do you think conditions were worse for soldiers at Gallipoli than on the Western Front?

Desert Warfare

Turkey joined the war as Germany's ally in October 1914. The Ottoman Empire of Turkey controlled and governed much of the Middle East and was therefore in a position to cut off supplies of the Middle East oil on which Britain depended. Not only that, but Turkey also had power over Egypt and could seal off the Suez Canal. This would cut Britain's main sea route to Australia and India. Without help and supplies from her Empire, Britain would find it difficult to continue the war in Europe. In view of these dangers, Britain sent armies to Palestine and Iraq — then known as Mesopotamia.

Lawrence of Arabia. Why do you think Lawrence adopted Arab dress? What can you find out about the life of Lawrence of Arabia?

The Palestine and Mesopotamia campaigns were much more difficult to fight than the war in Europe. The desert war was fought across huge distances, making the job of supplying the troops a nightmare. In the summer season, supplies of drinking water had to be rationed. The terrain was hostile, too. There were few landmarks and fewer reliable maps. Perhaps the biggest problem of all was the fact that the best equipment and weaponry were sent to the Western Front, leaving the armies in the Middle East to make do with antiquated weapons and shortage of supplies.

LAWRENCE OF ARABIA

A British army was sent to Palestine to protect the Suez Canal. The Palestine campaign is remembered chiefly for the heroic deeds of Colonel T.E. Lawrence – Lawrence of Arabia. Lawrence helped to organize an underground resistance movement amongst the Arabs, against the Turks who governed their country. He managed to persuade the Arab tribes to stop fighting one another and to start fighting for national independence.

Lawrence persuaded General Allenby, Commander of the British Forces, to keep the Arab fighters supplied with arms and explosives. In Arab costume himself, he led countless raiding parties on Turkish supply lines, his main target being the Hijaz railway. This guerilla warfare succeeded where direct attacks would have failed. The Turks had to divert many valuable troops from the front line to hunt down Lawrence's Arab raiders. Britain was grateful to her newly-found allies and when the war was over, played an important part in helping to set up the emerging Arab states.

In his book, *Seven Pillars of Wisdom*, Lawrence relates his experience of a camel charge:

The Imperial Camel Corps gallop into action. Would armoured vehicles have been more effective?

THE THIRD BATTLE OF GAZA

The following extract from a soldier's diary describes the third battle of Gaza, in Palestine:

Nasir screamed at me, 'Come on' with his bloody mouth; and we plunged our camels madly over the hill, and down towards the head of the fleeing enemy. The slope was not too steep for a camel-gallop, but steep enough to make their pace terrific, and their course uncontrollable: yet the Arabs were able to extend to right and left and to shoot into the Turkish brown. The Turks had been too bound up in the terror of Auda's furious charge against their rear to notice us as we came over the eastward slope: so we took them by surprise and in the flank; and a charge of ridden camels going nearly thirty miles an hour was irresistible. (T.E. Lawrence, *Seven Pillars of Wisdom*, Jonathan Cape, 1935)

What advantages did camels have in desert warfare?

Wednesday 31/10/1917   Gaza

Breakfast – bacon, biscuits, tea and rum, jam. Guns going, whizzing through the air as I write this. . . . Shrapnel is bursting in our Waddi. . . .

. . . Stupid to be in front of these guns which are banging away all the time, kicking up hell's delight and drawing fire which we are catching. Ground hard and stony. Crouch down and keep shifting after each shell. First up, then down, then sideways. A man is guarding the pack dump (we dumped packs). A shell explodes very near him but he sat there with his fixed bayonet as cool as if reclining on a mossy bank. Ordered to move. More shells. Call for stretcher bearers . . . .

Our own guns give a bang followed by another and we are smothered with flying bits. A premature burst from our guns 200 yards away. Cries of 'that's got us'. Several casualties. One fellow (Rogers) jaw all blown to fragments, blood spattering from nose. Gives one or two heaves. Is bound up but expires and is carried away . . . (Private D.H. Calcutt, Queen's Westminster Rifles)

The Western Front – the Trenches

TRENCH LAYOUT

The following extract from an officer's letter explains very clearly the layout of the trenches occupied by his battalion (1000 men). This sort of information is rarely found in letters from servicemen and the letter contains information that could have been of vital importance to the enemy. Officers were trusted to censor their own letters. It is lucky that this one did not fall into the wrong hands!

The early months of the war had seen armies on the move across northern Europe. The war of movement stopped in late 1914 when the Germans and the Allies dug lines of trenches to defend the positions they held. The trenches stretched all the way from the Swiss border to the Belgian coast.

B.E.F. 16 .2. 16

A battalion holds about 800 to 1000 yards of front-line trench, as a rule (that is, supposing it to be up to full strength), and of course is also responsible for the depth behind the front line. A sector of trench is rather like this:

You must understand that it is in reality nothing so regular as this; the 'communications trenches,' for instance, connecting up the different lines, it would be madness to dig as straight as I have shown, as a sniper would shoot right down the length of them. They are also much more numerous: and in addition there are

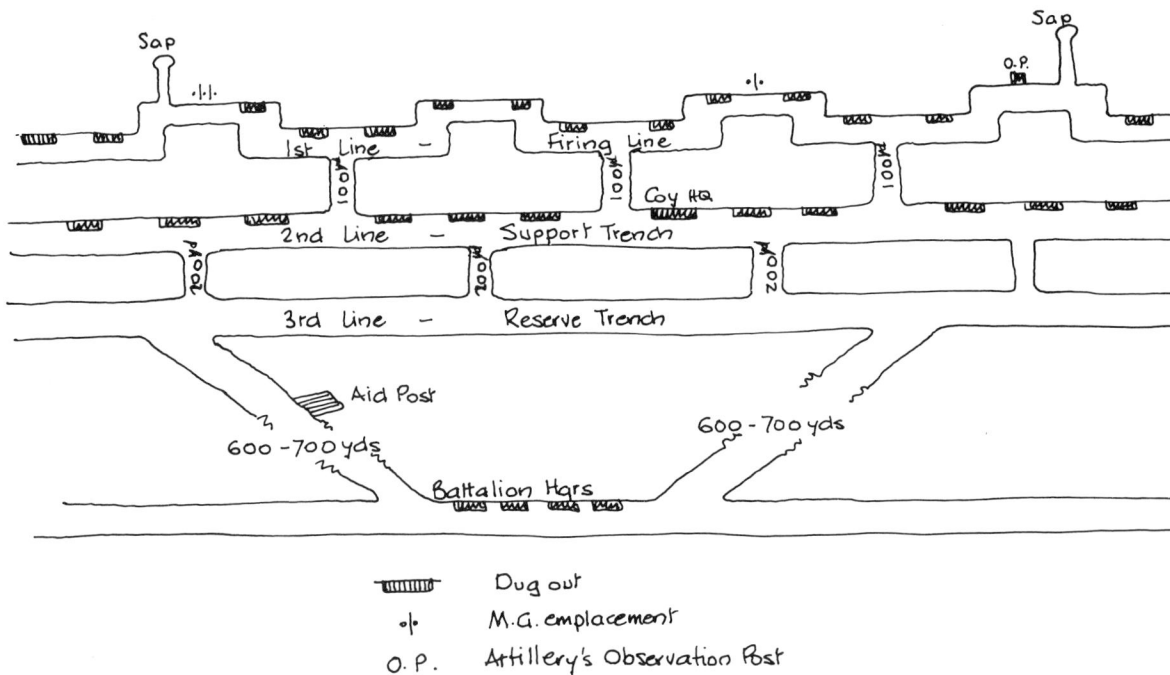

Sap

Sap

O.P.

1st Line – Firing Line

100 yards

Coy HQ

2nd Line – Support Trench

200 yards

3rd Line – Reserve Trench

Aid Post

600 -700 yds

600 - 700 yds

Battalion Hqrs

Dug out
•|•	M.G. emplacement
O. P.	Artillery's Observation Post

Men fix bayonets as they prepare to go into battle. The hut on the left surrounded by sandbags is a ▷ command post.

lots of little blind alleys for latrines, and old disused trenches and things.

Three of the battalion's four companies hold a section each of the front line – Right, Centre and Left companies – and they usually select a dug-out in the Support Trench for their headquarters. The fourth company goes in reserve, right back somewhere near Battalion HQ. In the same way the four platoons in each company dispose themselves: three in the firing-line, and one behind them in support. The front line is garrisoned as thinly as possible, to avoid shell-casualties: a few men in each fire-bay with rifles and periscopes, and the rest of the garrison in their dug-outs, where they can be called out instantly – leaving their rifles loaded standing on the parapet all ready. The saps (projecting short trenches running out towards the enemy) are garrisoned with bombers as well as riflemen. And at intervals along the front line are carefully sandbagged emplacements for machine-guns. (The point I have marked 'O.P.' is an artillery observation post, where the gunners send an officer to control the fire of their battery somewhere away behind a hill, to which he is connected by telephone.)

Away back, a thousand yards or so, is a collection of superior wooden dug-outs at Battalion HQ; one perhaps for the C.O. and Adjutant, one for the 2nd-in-Command and Doctor, one for the signal office, one for the orderly room, and so on. (Personally, I double in with the Doctor.) (Letters of Captain Maxwell Staniforth, Connaught Rangers)

HOME FROM HOME

Saturday 24 April 1915

We are between Marble Arch and Ludgate Hill. This *may* sound odd and must be explained. At various places it has been found necessary to build archways covered with sandbags to prevent enfilading. At various other places there are pathways leading up from the dead ground behind the fire trench. And at another point a small ditch cuts our lines. . . . Thus Ludgate Hill is one of the steep paths. Westminster Bridge is the bridge over the ditch; Southend Pier is the wooden pathway through the mud at the rear of the trenches. (Diaries of Private Frank Minter, Queen's Westminster Rifles)

Why do you think soldiers named their trenches after familiar British landmarks or London streets?

Soldiers also used to give English-sounding equivalents to the names of the foreign towns they passed through. For example, Ploegsteert was called "Plug Street". Can you find out nicknames for any other towns in Flanders or northern France?

What was the most effective weapon to defend a trench with? What weapons were used to bombard the enemy trenches? Why were telephones important in trench warfare? What do you think was the purpose of sandbags around the machine gun emplacements?

The Trenches – Support Line Duties

A WIRING PARTY

One of the duties of troops in support was to maintain the defences. In the following extract from his *Memoirs*, Lieutenant Armfield describes how barbed wire entanglements were repaired:

A wiring party usually comprising about a dozen men under a sergeant would collect rolls of barbed wire, piquet posts, wire cutters, protective gloves etc from the nearby dump and would leave the front line trench from a point as near as possible to the section of wire entanglement to be repaired. Even in the darkness one felt singularly prominent standing in the open beside the wire in no-man's-land. The work had to be done as quietly as possible – no easy task when unwinding rusty barbed wire from reels and attaching it to the metal piquet posts which had first to be driven in to the ground and then screwed into the soil until they had become firmly fixed. Speed of work and personal safety were dependent on the distance between the two front lines. In some places, this was only about 75 yards. The Germans might become suspicious of noise and fire a Verey light. As soon as the flare rose from the trench, every member of the wiring party instantly became and remained absolutely rigid in whatever position he might at that moment be in – the least movement would be seen in the bright light of the rocket and most likely followed at once by a burst of machine gun fire. (2nd Lieutenant Armfield, 2/4 Battalion, London Regiment)

Trench warfare was a waiting game. Battles were few and far between, but each side had to be constantly on the alert in case of enemy attack. During the daytime, snipers (marksmen with rifles) were watching and waiting for targets to shoot at. Both sides often had a regular time at which they would begin pounding the other's trenches with shell and mortar fire for an hour or so. This was called "morning hate". At night there was also the danger of lightning attacks, and raiding parties were sometimes sent out to surprise the enemy and bring back prisoners for questioning.

Troops in the support line trenches played a vital part in bringing up supplies and food rations to the front. They not only faced enemy fire but were also given backbreaking and often dangerous jobs to do – as the extracts here show.

Wiring party at work. You can see Verey lights being fired in the background.

A WORK PARTY

Frank Minter tells a funny story of a work party detailed to carry planks of wood from a supply dump to the front line trenches. The planks were needed to shore up an underground sap that was being dug towards the enemy trenches.

Thursday 29.4.15 Poetzje

Now plank carrying is not easy. The rifle is slung across the back over the right shoulder and under the left arm. Thus I carried the plank on my left shoulder. This got frightfully tired, but under the arm was a worse way than that and not so steady. The planks were very long; 15 feet. The ends constantly collided with other ends and trees and, not infrequently, with other men's heads. The ground was rough and more than once I saw a white plank bobbing along in front of me suddenly sink to the ground to the accompaniment of a few army swear words. Add to this that we were near enough to the trenches to have a few bullets whizz by . . . . We followed a broad pathway through a thin wood until reaching the fringe of the latter we found the reserve trenches . . . .

We were now quite near the firing line and could hear our own men talking now and then, when suddenly a stage whisper reached us: "Here, I say", and a figure bent double ran towards us. "Hallo", said our officer. "What the devil are you doing with those planks?" said the figure. "The officer at the dumping ground sent them to captain Z". "I'm captain Z and half an hour ago I sent those planks back to the dumping ground. They're what we had over from mining. Of all the . . . etc etc." He knew quite a lot about the English language did that officer but he would have learnt a lot more if he had been able to hear some of our remarks. (Diaries of Private Frank Minter, Queen's Westminster Rifles)

Once again, work is being carried out at night. Why do you think most support line duties were carried out at this time? What difficulties might the men encounter when they worked at night?

COLLECTING THE FOOD RATIONS

Each regiment was responsible for distributing food, munitions and supplies to its battalions in the field. Horse-drawn limbers (wagons) were used to transport materials from central supply dumps which were usually sited at main railway stations well behind the line of battle.

We took turns going back for rations. Each company formed its own party. One or two men from each section. Single file, we would leave the support lines and make for a rendezvous about three miles back, where we would meet the regimental transport wagons that had come up under cover of darkness, laden with sand-bags filled with food. These were dumped as quickly as possible on the wagons drawn by horses that seemed to scent the need for quietness and would glide off into the night. Each bag usually held enough food for a dozen men. Lumps of cheese, bacon, about three loaves of bread, tins of bully-beef, and a supply of cigarettes. This was all divided up when we got back to the trenches. Sometimes there was no bread, sometimes no cigarettes, and sometimes we had the journey for nothing, for there would be no arrival of the transport wagons: And so the boys went hungry. The journey back for rations was not a job to crave after. It took the best part of the night, for three miles in the darkness across broken country, with shell holes full of water every few yards, the enemy searching the ground with shrapnel shells, and always the danger of getting hopelessly lost, made it a trek that none of us cared about; And we invariably returned with less men than we started off with. (Memoirs of Private William Quinton, 4th Battalion, Bedfordshire Regiment)

Into Battle

Trenches were very difficult to attack because to reach them, soldiers had to pick their way through barbed wire obstacles and charge across no-man's-land where they could be easily mown down by enemy artillery and machine guns. In the notorious Battle of the Somme 20,000 British soldiers were killed and 40,000 were wounded in the first attack which took place on 1 July 1916.

GOING OVER THE TOP

"Going over the top" was the expression used to describe the infantry climbing out of the shelter of their trenches and rushing across no-man's-land to attack the enemy lines. It was a nerve-wracking experience, as this account shows.

Bouchavesnes   1 Sept 1918

The first faint lights of dawn were just breaking in the distant western sky. In the grey light I stood in the trench looking at my wrist watch .... I watched the minute hand moving slowly on to 5.30 a.m. then drawing my revolver, I called out, 'Here we go lads!' and clambered out of the trench followed by my platoon, well aware that wherever I went they would faithfully follow for as long as they could stand on their feet ...

Attack formation at this time was in 'blobs', small sections or parties of 4 or 5 men moving forward at walking pace at about 25 yards interval from each other. Thus if one section was held up the others would go forward independently under their own section leader. There was no cover whatever; even had there been we were not expected to take advantage of it – that was implicit in the provision of a creeping barrage. The troops were expected to move forward steadily to their objective or until shot down or halted temporarily by heavy machine guns or other fire from directly ahead when sections on right or left would continue to advance and bring fire to bear from the flanks to the enemy's point of resistance.

Soon after leaving the assembly trench and advancing over the open gently rising ground, a 'runner' came forward to report to me that a single shell had wiped out the Company Commander (2nd Lieutenant Prince) and his entire headquarters party, and that I was now in command. I acknowledged the message and continued to advance with my platoon. In my right hand I carried a drawn revolver, my single offensive weapon. The men carried rifles with fixed bayonets, each platoon including a Lewis gun section. (*Memoirs* of 2nd Lieutenant Armfield, 2/4 Battalion, London Regiment)

Lieutenant Armfield was aged about 20 at the time of this incident. Do you think he was too young to take so much responsibility? Why do you think it was common for officers to be very young? Why did the infantry carry rifles with fixed bayonets?

GAS ATTACK

In this extract William Quinton describes the German gas attack of 1 May 1915, at the second battle of Ypres, when the Germans retook Hill 60 that had been captured by the British a month earlier. Gas had been first used as an offensive weapon that same year, on 22 April, near Ypres. The British were quick to copy the idea. Although silent, gas was feared and hated by the infantry. Its effects were more dreadful than those of shellfire as it caused a long, lingering and very unpleasant death.

Suddenly over the top of our front line we saw what looked like clouds of thin grey smoke rolling slowly along with the slight wind. It hung to the ground reaching to the height of 8 or 9 ft, and approaching so slowly that a man walking could have kept ahead of it. Gas! The word quickly passed round. Even now it held no terror for us, for we had not yet tasted it. From our haversacks we hastily drew the flannel belts, soaked them in water and tied them round our mouths and noses . . . .

Suddenly through the communication trench came rushing a few khaki-clad figures. Their eyes glaring out of their heads, their hands tearing at their throats, they came on. Some stumbled and fell, and lay writhing in the bottom of the trench, choking and gasping, whilst those following trampled over them. If ever men were raving mad with terror, these men were. (Private William Quinton, 4th Battalion, Bedfordshire Regiment)

What do you think was so terrifying about a gas attack? Find out how the British army tried to overcome the threat of gas attacks.

ARTILLERY FIRE

An artillery barrage was used before a battle to knock holes in the barbed wire entanglements of no-man's-land and to weaken enemy resistance. Sometimes, though, artillery fire was simply used to play upon the nerves of the opposing side and demoralize them.

Northern France 29.12.1915
Their heavy shells make a fine noise coming over, though; just like a railway train, pounding along through the sky quite slowly. . . .

And the keynote of the whole thing is boredom and weariness, utter and absolute. You sit in a dug out and read or play cards from morning till night, and your nerves get worn out with watching against Hun attacks which never come and with shoring up parapets that crumble in even as you dig, and pumping out water that fills up again as fast as you can get it out.
(Letters of Captain Maxwell Staniforth, Connaught Rangers)

Would you have preferred to take part in an attack or to have sat in a trench for days or weeks on end? Which situation would give you the highest chances of survival do you think?

British soldier wearing an early type of gas mask. It is ▷ an improvement on the flannel belt soaked in water described by Private Quinton, but how effective do you think it would be in a gas attack?

Trench Life

Even without an enemy firing at you, living in a trench was dangerous and unhealthy. In wet weather, trenches would fill up with water and men would have to wade through mud that was sometimes waist-deep.

When an advance had been made and a new piece of land won from the enemy, fresh trenches had to be dug – often on the very battlefield itself. In his autobiography, *Goodbye to All That*, written in 1929, Robert Graves remembers trenches that were dug through half-buried human remains. In one such trench a leg sticking out of the parapet was used by a soldier as a rifle rest until an officer made him hack it off.

It is not surprising that rats fed on the corpses that were littered around and helped to spread a killer disease called typhus.

KEEPING CLEAN

Richard Plint was nineteen years old when he joined the army in Liverpool in 1915. As a bank employee, he was eligible to join the specially formed "Bankers' Battalion" of the Royal Fusiliers. This was one of the special "pals" battalions formed to attract volunteers with similar backgrounds and interests.

In this extract from his memoirs written in 1967, Mr Plint describes one of the luxuries of life in the reserve line at Ploegsteert:

Washing was always difficult. When we occupied Fosse Labarre we drew water from the moat and if not on duty at the time we also bathed in it. It was green and a large bullfrog lived in it ....

Other sources of water were shell holes and shaving was often done with the remains of the tea ....

Bathing usually meant a change of underclothing. Each man had a complete change – vest, shirt, pants (long or short) and socks which he took with him and put on after the bath. The dirty garments were handed in and a clean change received in exchange. The dirty clothes were all 'stoved' in a big container in the hope that the heat would kill the lice .... Lice could not be avoided no matter how careful one was .... 'Long johns' were a breeding ground and we got rid of them in exchange as soon as possible. Vests were not too bad but the seams of shirts were a happy hunting ground: we usually scorched them with a candle flame to burn out the fluff in which the lice laid their eggs. Sometimes the seams would go off like a tiny machine gun. (Richard Plint, MM, Corporal, 26th "Bankers' Battalion", Royal Fusiliers)

The ordinary French soldier was known as a "poilu" (hairy) because he never bothered to shave regularly. Why did the British troops consider washing and shaving to be so important?

Do you know what puttees were? How did they help keep a soldier's trousers from getting muddy?

◁ *Foot inspection by the medical officer of the 12th East Yorkshires, January 1918. "Trench feet" was caused by wearing tight boots for days in cold, wet conditions. In severe cases, blood circulation stopped and the foot had to be amputated to prevent infection from spreading.*

Cigarettes were smoked almost universally in the army. Many brands offered discounts to troops and cigarettes were also given to the men as part of their army rations. ▷

THE 'TANK' COMMANDER

THE 'SUB'

"O.T.C."

DESPATCH RIDER

THE CAPTAIN

THE R.F.C.

THE 'MAJOR'
(soliloquising)
"Quite a discriminating fellow our new Captain... said he could offer me a better cigarette than I was smoking. Jove he was right too... A man who can find out a good thing like this won't be long before he gets his majority... must make a note to get some. What's the name?.. Ah!"

THE "OBSERVATION" OFFICER

"CAVANDER'S CIGARETTES"

20 for 9d.   50 for 1/10.   100 for 3/9.

SLEEPING QUARTERS

France 29.12.1916

The dug-out itself, which was twenty feet below the surface, gave one the impression of being in a coal mine. There were the same enormous pit props shoring up the roof, the same eternal drip, drip, drip from the ceiling, and the same heavy atmosphere and absolute silence. It was about as big as your bathroom, and six of us slept there: one on the table, one under it, the Colonel on his bed (a hospital stretcher, raised on two trestles) another under that, and two of us side by side on the floor.

After I had dumped my things down, I went out to explore the front line. The water in some places was up to the thighs and nowhere under the ankles; the wet walls of the trench smeared one all over as you pushed along between them; so you can believe that when men come out after four days on duty there is absolutely nothing to be seen of man, uniform, cap, equipment, face or rifle. And the mud is of every consistency from thin gravel that is half water to the stiff gluey clay that pulls the boots off your legs. (Letters of Captain Maxwell Staniforth, Connaught Rangers)

Duckboards were used by the army to try to overcome the problem of water-filled trenches. Find out what they looked like and how they were used.

RATS

Sunday December 3rd 1916

Amount of rats about in the night. They frequently make excursions about your body. In one of the dug-outs the other night, two men sat smoking by the light of a candle very quiet – all at once candle moved and flickered. Looking up they saw that a rat was dragging it away – fact. (Diary of Lieutenant Frank Bass, 23rd Battalion, Middlesex Regiment)

Can you suggest some methods that the soldiers could have used to combat the problem of rats? Could the rats ever have been got rid of in the trenches?

Contact with Home

Servicemen and their relatives were able to post letters to one another for the cheap rate of one penny. Parcels were slightly dearer to send. The amount of mail that could be sent was unlimited.

Before a man on active service could send a letter it had first to be read by an officer to check that it did not mention place names or give information that could be useful to the enemy. This was called censoring.

When they wanted to address a letter, relatives could write only a man's name, his regiment or ship and the country in which he was serving. One witty soldier was able to fool the censor and let his parents know where he was stationed by addressing his letters home to a non-existent person by the name of Y.P. Rees (Ypres). When he was moved to Poperinghe his next letter was to a certain Mr P.O. Perring!

GALLANT ATTEMPT BY A MEMBER OF THE BRITISH EXPEDITIONARY FORCE TO DO JUSTICE TO ALL HIS NEW YEAR'S GIFTS.

LETTER FROM A MOTHER

44 Milligan Road
Leicester
Sunday 9 Sept 1917

Dear Friend,

I am addressing you as a friend as any friend of my Boy's is my friend. I thank you for sending us word of how our dear Ernest died. We had also a very nice letter from the captain the day before we received yours. It is a dreadful thought to lose our Dear Boy in this way. We would not believe it till we had a letter from someone who saw him.

Did you see my boy after he died, could you tell us how he was? I should like to know what time of the day or night it happened (or thereabouts). Was he up the doings (are you allowed to tell us?) or was he on Sentry?

I am sure we are all the while thinking of you dear lads, hoping and praying for you to be kept safe, and when these Awful tidings are sent us it shakes our faith. But then again when we get calm we know that God is still in his heaven and He orders all things for the best. I sent Ernie a parcel off on 21 August; if you should see anything of it, will you share out what is good between you and your friends. I shall never forget you and hope you will write often to me. So thank you I close

Yours truly, Mrs Gay

(Sent to Private J.S. Smith, Northern

◁ *A cartoon from* Punch, *January 1915, shows how generously people gave to the fighting troops abroad. Because postage was cheap, anxious parents were able to send regular parcels of food and other useful items like knitted socks and balaclava helmets.*

◁ An embroidered postcard sent home by a soldier in France. Nowadays these cards are collectors' items and you can often find them in antique fairs or junk shops.

Children were encouraged to "adopt" a lonely soldier or sailor. They would then save up their pocket money in order to send small presents. These children's presents were collected and given out to the men in most need. This certificate was given to a child who had sent a Christmas gift to a member of the armed forces.

Cyclist Corps, quoted in Lyn Macdonald, *They Called it Passchendaele*, Michael Joseph, 1978)

When a soldier was killed, his commanding officer had to write to his next of kin to inform them. What would you have written to Mrs Gay if you had been her son's C.O.?

A THANK YOU LETTER

Gunner H.A. Buttle 95181
B Battery 148 Brigade
RFA
BEF   France
24/4/1919

Dear Miss Lucy,

I now take the great pleasure of writing these few lines to you just to thank you for the socks and the knitted comforter [scarf]. I hope you are in the best of health as it leaves me the same at present. I think that it is through thinking about nice little girls like you that has helped us beat the Germans. Well, you will not have to worry about air raids now, that is one thing. Well dear Miss Lucy I shall soon be a civilian again but if I can find a nice little present out here be sure you shall get it just to show me and my chums appreaciate [sic] your little kindness to us this is all I have to say at present so must close with kindest thanks from my chums and me.

I remain
yours gratefully
Gunner H.A. Buttle

(From Bequest of Miss Lucy Bateson, Imperial War Museum)

How did contact with home improve the morale of the fighting men? Do you think it was a good idea to involve children in sending presents to soldiers and sailors? Would this have made them more aware of the war?

Morale

...important to keep the morale of the ...ghting men high. A war could not be won by tired and dispirited troops. But fighting, especially in front line trenches, was often horrifying and cruel. Death and wounding were so common that men simply came to terms with them and carried on their daily life. In front line trenches fires and singing were forbidden because they gave away troop positions to the enemy, allowing them to direct their fire effectively. But the men could sing and be merry when they had a chance. Troops spent only a limited amount of time in the trenches and weeks at a time were often spent away from the front lines.

Men were given regular leave to visit local towns. In their spare time men wrote home, and food parcels and letters from Britain arrived regularly. No matter how bad the war, human nature somehow managed to find the bright side.

"Where did that one go?"

◁ Old Bill and his two chums have a lucky escape. Old Bill was the cartoon creation of Captain Bruce Bairnsfather of the Warwickshire Regiment. With his walrus moustache, balaclava helmet, clay pipe and muffler, Old Bill aways survived to live another day.

THE WIPERS TIMES

Our paper was started as the result of the discovery of an old printing house just off the square at Wipers (Ypres). *Some* printing house and *some* square! There were parts of the building remaining, the rest was on top of the press ....

One of our sergeants, by nature an optimist and in a previous existence a printer, said he could make the press print if he had a brace of light duty men to help him. He got them, and was as good as his word as, within three or four days, be brought me a specimen of his handiwork.

Paper was there, ink in plenty, everything in fact except 'copy'. As none of us were writing men we just wrote down any old thing that came into our heads. Little incidents of daily life in the Salient were turned into adverts or small paragraphs ....

Have you ever sat in the middle of a battle and corrected proofs? Try it. That is what happened on the Somme, and the 'Somme Times' was the result. The paper has never yet been printed out of the front area, and once our works were within 700 yards of the front line and *above ground.* (From a facsimile edition of collected issues of *The Wipers Times*, published by Herbert Jenkins, 1918)

Letters and advertisements from the Wipers Times. *What was the purpose of this newspaper, do you think? (It was renamed the* Somme Times *when the people who produced it were moved to the Somme.)*

OH! IT'S A LOVELY WAR

Up to your waist in water, up to your
    eyes in slush
Using the kind of language, that makes
    the sergeant blush;
Who wouldn't join the army? that's
    what we all enquire,
Don't we pity the poor civilians sitting
    beside the fire.
Chorus
Oh! Oh! Oh! it's a lovely war,
Who wouldn't be a soldier eh?
Oh! it's a shame to take the pay.
As soon as "reveille" has gone
We feel just as heavy as lead,
But we never get up till the sergeant
    brings
Our breakfast up to bed.
Oh! Oh! Oh! it's a lovely war,
What do we want with eggs and ham
When we've got plum and apple jam?
Form fours! right turn!
How shall we spend the money we
    earn?
Oh! Oh! Oh! it's a lovely war.

When does the soldier grumble? when
    does he make a fuss?
No one is more contented in all the
    world than us;
Oh! it's a cushy life, boys, really we
    love it so
Once a fellow was sent on leave and
    simply refused to go.
Chorus.

Come to the cookhouse door boys, sniff
    at the lovely stew.
Who is it says the Colonel gets better
    grub than you?
Any complaints this morning? do we
    complain? not we.
What's the matter with lumps of onion
    floating around the tea?
Chorus
(By J.P. Long and Maurice Scott)
(© 1917 Reproduced by permission of EMI
Music Publishing Ltd London WC2H 0LD)

What do you learn about a soldier's life from this song? What makes "Oh! It's a Lovely War" funny? Do you know any other popular First World War songs?

Feeding an Army

Feeding an army on the battlefield was a difficult problem. Large quantities of food had to be ordered and brought up to the front line, usually in horse-drawn limbers.

FOOD SHORTAGES

Some front line positions were difficult to keep supplied with fresh food and men had to rely on their "iron rations" – hard biscuits and corned beef (the famous "bully beef"). The notorious "plum and apple" jam was always in plentiful supply.

When not on look-out, our time was our own. We had breakfast. Cooking it was a tedious job. About a quarter of an hour to get a mess tin of water to boil over a small fire made of twigs, or with no fire at all, but just the flames of a couple of candles. Sometimes when the water was nearly boiling, an enemy shell dropping near at hand would send over clouds of mud, and it was a hundred to one that a lump of mud would find its way into the water or the mess tin *and* water would be knocked over in the scramble for safety. We managed to sizzle our meagre supply of bacon in a mess tin lid. The chief meal of the day was always the one in which we included our rasher of bacon, whether it be at 3 pm. or 3 am. Otherwise it was bread and jam or bread and cheese, and not much of it at that. It is surprising how small an amount of food a man can live on and still remain healthy. A 2lb loaf between four men was the usual ration to last two to three days.

A field canteen in northern France, October 1916. How were the stoves moved from place to place, do you think?

Armentières, May 1916. A French woman pours coffee for some off-duty soldiers.

Army biscuits kept the worms from biting, but even these were very scarce sometimes, and a man who had a hoard of them could always barter them at about ten cigarettes per biscuit when there was a shortage of food. Jam was usually fairly plentiful. I have often seen men eat up a pound of tinned jam with their spoon when no other food was at hand. When we had no sugar, jam came in very useful for sweetening the tea. (Memoirs of Private William Quinton, 4th Battalion, Bedfordshire Regiment)

What do you think were the conditions that could have led to shortages of food at the front line? At which times of the year would the soldiers have been given more fresh food? What were the advantages of tinned food?

MAKING THE BEST OF IT

Food was always an item of interest. In the line, cooking was difficult as no smoke could be made. Charcoal was used for heating and I think our cooks did well considering everything. They had to learn their job. No doubt the continued outdoor life sharpened our appetites but I still remember one 'Plug Street' dinner – roast shoulder of lamb, roast potatoes, peas and gravy – all perfectly cooked. As I have already mentioned, we bought food at the canteen and cooked something extra for supper over the primus stove. When the latter packed up we used 'Tommy Cookers' or small tins of fat .... The oil from fried cheese etc would be used to supplement the fat and the smell was unbelievable but the result was usually worth eating. (Memoirs of

TINNED FOOD

A tin of Maconochie's consisted of meat, potatoes, beans and other vegetables and could be eaten cold, but we generally used to fry them up in the tin on a fire.

. . . But another firm that supplied them at this time must have made enormous profits out of the British Government. Before ever we opened the first tins that were supplied by them we smelt a rat. The name of the firm made us suspicious. When we opened them our suspicions were well-founded. There was nothing inside but a rotten piece of meat and some boiled rice. The head of that firm should have been put against the wall and shot for the way they sharked us troops. (Private Frank Richards, DCM, MM, 2nd Battalion, Royal Welsh Fusiliers, quoted in *Old Soldiers Never Die* published by Faber and Faber, 1933, reprinted by permission of Faber and Faber Ltd)

The tinned food described in this extract was supplied by a private company with a government contract. Why would some firms have been given a contract to supply food?

Richard Plint MM, Corporal, 26th Battalion, Royal Fusiliers)

Why was it important to use smokeless fuel like charcoal near the front line? Why do you think soldiers bought extra food with their army pay? Do you know how a primus stove works?

Injury and Death

I crouch in behind some infantry holes (I won't call them shelters) and while there, one of them is carried in. The top of his head is lifted off, a clean swipe whatever got him. One (his chum I expect) holds his hand, and I see him die. The first for me to see die, as they say, for his country. And it might be glorious, noble, brave, heroic and all the rest of those beautiful words that sound so well on a platform or toasting your toes by the fireside, but it certainly is not a glorious sight to see a young fellow, with his face covered with blood stiffening out in a hole dug out of clay.

Millions of lives were lost in the First World War. The account given by George Harbottle of the attack on St Julien (page 10-11) will give you some idea of the huge numbers of casualties that could be reported after a day's fighting in just one sector of the Western Front.

Injury and death were a fact of everyday life and the men who fought became hardened to suffering. Each man must have believed in his own luck and that somehow he would survive in spite of the odds.

It isn't glorious, it's murder, was my thoughts when I saw my first infantryman die. (Memoirs of Gunner Hiram Sturdy, Royal Artillery)

Why does Gunner Sturdy call the soldier's death "murder"? Why do you think he is so emotional?

Face to face with the enemy. British and German side by side on stretchers outside a dressing station, August 1916. Would you have hated the enemy or felt sorry for wounded enemy soldiers?

◁ *A lucky escape. Shrapnel has pierced this soldier's helmet but left him unharmed. In the early years of the war men were issued only with soft caps.*

"A BLIGHTY ONE"

A "Blighty one" was the soldiers' name for a wound that was not serious enough to kill you but was enough to ensure that you would be sent back to Britain ("Blighty") for hospital treatment. A permanent disability might lead to a soldier's being discharged from the army as unfit for military duty.

> **Suddenly I felt a terrific blow on my right arm, just as if somebody had hit me on the funny-bone as hard as he could with a sledge-hammer. It spun me round like a top and I collapsed in the bottom of the trench. The man next to me rolled over and said, 'You ain't 'alf bloody well got 'it in the 'and, sir!' and on looking down I saw that my right hand was a mass of blood.**
>
> **My arm still felt numb from the blow, and I could hardly realise that it was my hand that was hit, as it did not hurt at all. However, this man cut my field dressing out of my tunic, and after dousing my hand with iodine, which *did* hurt, he bound it up very well; he then made a sling out of my woollen scarf which I was wearing, insisted on giving me one of his own cigarettes and lighting it for me, and told me not to worry, I was 'for Blighty all right with that packet!' This sounded too good to be true and I felt distinctly better.**
> (Memoirs of Captain Jack Needham, Northamptonshire Regiment)

THE DEATH OF AN ENEMY SOLDIER

I jumped down into the German trench followed by an NCO whose name I now forget, and about eight men. The trench was deserted except for some bodies of dead Germans. Later I noticed the sad manner of the death of one of these. Evidently a piece of shell had carried away the whole calf of his leg, baring it to the bone. He had dragged half of his body into a cubby hole at the bottom of the trench there to die quietly, in the dark, his face hidden from the world. He was respected and grieved for in death by at least one enemy soldier. (Memoirs of 2nd Lieutenant Armfield, 2/4 Battalion, London Regiment)

Lieutenant Armfield "respected and grieved for" the enemy soldier. Do you find this strange? What would your reactions have been?

All soldiers carried a dressing and a small bottle of iodine in their tunic. Why do you think it was useful to give immediate first aid to casualties? Why do you think Captain Needham felt "distinctly better" at the thought of being sent back to Britain?

Cowardice and Desertion

The British army was well-disciplined and, generally, morale was high throughout the war. But there were a growing number of cases of self-inflicted wounds and of desertion. In 1914, for example, there were only 409 deserters; in 1917 the figure stood at 21,871.

Military crimes would be dealt with by courts martial. At the front line a court martial was often a very hurried affair. There were no lawyers and the young officers who acted as defence, prosecution and judge were usually unsympathetic. If found guilty, a soldier received often severe punishment. In extreme cases, soldiers were sentenced to death by firing squad. Of the 3,080 death sentences passed, only 346 were carried out, according to War Office statistics.

FALSELY ACCUSED OF COWARDICE

Many men were in what were called reserved occupations. This meant that it was actually against the law for them to enlist for military service. Among the reserved occupations were civil servants, coal miners and railwaymen. Some men in reserved occupations wanted to join up so badly that they ran away to distant towns to enlist. Some even changed their names. Although these men were breaking the law, no action was ever taken against them.

The following story was told by a 92-year-old war veteran who had been born and brought up in the mining village of Ashington in Northumberland.

I was wounded in March 1916 and after a long time in hospitals was sent home on class W, which meant I could be called up at any time. My brother Tom had joined up with the Royal Naval Division and was fighting with the land forces in Flanders.

When I went home, our youngest brother Nichol was only 18. He was working down a coal mine so was reserved.

One morning at breakfast, Nichol received a letter, opened it, and a white feather dropped out. His face went pale, but he never spoke. He got up from the table, went upstairs, came down dressed, and went out. I never saw him again.

That night, I asked mother where he was and she said he had gone to join up in the army.

Some months later, my parents received a visit from the Salvation Army to say that brother Tom was in hospital in France severely wounded. The Salvation Army made all the arrangements for them to visit him, so I went down with them as far as London. I went to the War Office and obtained permission for our brother Nichol who was with the Durham Light Infantry to leave his unit and go to visit Tom in hospital while our parents were there.

Mother and father were at the hospital for some ten days while Tom was on the mend. Nichol stayed for four days, then had to return to his unit. While on his way back up a communication trench to the front line he was killed. (Sergeant Jack Dorgan, MM, 7th Battalion, Northumberland Fusiliers)

Jack Dorgan told me that some years after the war, the woman who had sent the white feather to his brother asked him if he would help her son get an apprenticeship in the engineering firm for which he was working. In Jack's own words, "I told her as gently as I could, the answer was no".

Dear Mr E A Brookes
Seeing that you cannot
be a man not to join
the Army. we offer you
an invitation to join our
Girl Scouts. as washer up.
Scoutmistress

BATH GIRL
SCOUTS

Mr E A Brookes
Porter
G W R
Bath

This example of a white feather letter was sent to a railway porter. The man would not have been able to join up because he was in a reserved occupation – a civilian job considered vital to the war effort. Who sent white feather letters and why?

DESERTION

With the terrible conditions of trench warfare, it is not surprising that men were sometimes tempted to run away. Lieutenant Armfield describes an encounter with a deserter:

> Around the bend in the trench a man came stumbling along the duckboards, cannoning off the moving soldiers on to the side of the trench and back again, his equipment clattering as he did so. I stood squarely in the middle of the trench and barred his way, stopping him in his tracks, the revolver barrel resting against his chest. 'Go back to your platoon!' I ordered. We stood motionless and silent, staring at each other. I repeated my order, 'go back to your platoon.' For a few moments, although it seemed longer, the soldier remained motionless, then slowly turned and retraced his steps along the trench towards the front line.
>
> God knows what I should have done if he had not obeyed the order. Shot him, I suppose. (Memoirs of 2nd Lieutenant Armfield, 2/4 Battalion, London Regiment)

What would you have done if you had been in Lieutenant Armfield's position and the soldier had disobeyed you? Was it fair to shoot deserters? What special reasons might a man have had to make him want to stop fighting?

Caring for the Sick and Wounded

During the war, field hospitals and dressing stations faced an ever-increasing burden in coping with battle casualties. British Army statistics reveal that just under half those who died in the First World War did so as a result of wounds or sickness. Field hospitals, of course, could not cope with the long-term care of the very badly injured. In the year up to 28 April 1918 the number of hospital cases evacuated from France averaged 23,420 per month.

FIRST AID

Doctors working at dressing stations and temporary hospitals near the front line of battle did a remarkable job of saving men's lives under the most difficult conditions imaginable. The speed of treating the wounded saved many needless deaths and sometimes gave men the chance to fight another day. Gunner Sturdy received his hand injury at Beaumont Hamel on the Somme on 3 July 1916.

I know of a first aid station close by, and make my way there. It is a glasshouse converted into a dressing station. I knock and hear a voice, 'Come in.' I enter and see two bare feet facing me. The doctor is leaning over the naked form of a man. He is taking little pieces out of his body. He is quiet. The doc turns round and asks me what I have got. I show him my hand, and he asks for my phial of iodine from my field dressing. I give it him. He opens the wound and empties the phial into it, points to a door, tells me to go down into the cellar for safety, and goes on picking at the naked man and Fritz shelling all over the place . . . .

As things quieten above, the doctor calls me up and tells me to make my way back. Back, that was all. (Memoirs of Gunner Hiram Sturdy, Royal Artillery)

Why do you think Gunner Sturdy was angry at the treatment he received?

A field dressing station. How was it possible for doctors to perform surgery under these conditions?

INSIDE A FIELD HOSPITAL

Vera Brittain's famous autobiography, *Testament of Youth*, describes her experiences as a VAD nurse. In the following extract she is describing her feelings at reading an official Red Cross report published after the war which claimed that VAD nurses were not "entrusted with trained nurses' work except on occasions when the emergency was so great that no other course was open."

... the incongruous picture came back to me of myself standing alone in a newly-created circle of hell during the 'emergency' of March 22nd 1918, and gazing, half hypnotised, at the dishevelled beds, the stretchers on the floor, the scattered boots and piles of muddy khaki, the brown blankets turned back from smashed limbs bound to splints by filthy blood-stained bandages. Beneath each stinking wad of sodden wool and gauze an obscene horror waited for me – and all the equipment that I had for attacking it in this ex-medical ward was one pair of forceps standing in a potted-meat glass half full of methylated spirit. (Vera Brittain, chapter 8/13, *Testament of Youth*, Victor Gollancz, 1933)

Could you have coped with the emergency described? What other drugs or equipment do you think would have been necessary to care for these wounded soldiers and relieve their suffering? What can you find out about the life of Vera Brittain?

A hospital train. Badly wounded troops were taken ▷ *from dressing stations to hospital in specially converted trains.*

MA

Matron was
sailed down
ward, and if
you stood ri
away.

Every mor
for uniform
including which was behaviour and how to behave on the wards – no showing of ankles. Black shoes and stockings, clean spotless apron, collar, cuffs and cap and on no account be familiar with a patient. Treat them well, look after them well, but eyes down and remember they have women folk of their own!! The rule – patient and nurse, must be definite – no talk of sex in those days – but we all understood the implications underlying Matron's instructions and advice. (Memoirs of Nurse D.M. Richards, VAD at Etaples)

The matron who inspected Nurse Richards evidently believed that discipline for its own sake was a good thing. What are your views on this subject? Do you think that there was any purpose behind First World War hospital regulations?

...ult Words

...icer who assists superiors with paper ...administration.

...countries which come to one another's aid in ...t of war.

bandolier leather shoulder strap containing ammunition pouches.

barracks place where soldiers live when on duty.

barrage heavy shellfire usually directed at a particular target.

battalion part of a regiment – 1,000 men.

battery a number of field guns gathered together in one place.

billet accommodation for a soldier in a civilian house.

Blighty Britain (comes from an Indian word for "home" – in popular use by the British Indian Army).

bomb often refers to a hand grenade.

brigade division of army, usually consisting of three battalions.

brigadier officer in charge of brigade.

bull ring parade ground.

bully beef corned beef in a tin.

captain commands a company of about 250 men.

column a line of troops marching.

company part of a battalion – 250 men.

conscript person directed to join armed forces.

convoy a group of ships or vehicles travelling together.

dressing station a first aid post.

duckboards narrow wooden rafts for bridging muddy holes or trenches.

enfilading shooting straight along a trench.

enlist to join the armed forces.

fatigues light duties.

firing line the outer trench facing the enemy across no-man's-land.

firing step raised ledge on the inside of trench on which soldiers can stand to shoot.

fusiliers originally, soldiers armed with light muskets.

garrison a soldier's base camp.

Guards the five top infantry regiments whose job it is to guard the Royal Household.

gunner rank in artillery equivalent of private.

iron rations emergency food supplies.

khaki greeny-brown colour of soldier's battledress.

lay a gun to align a field gun.

lieutenant in charge of a platoon.

limber small, horse-drawn cart on one axle, also part of a gun carriage.

major rank above captain in charge of one or more companies.

military service service in the army.

mills bomb type of hand grenade.

mobilize to recruit men and prepare them for immediate duty in the armed forces.

munitions military ammunition, equipment and stores.

national service period of duty in armed forces.

neutrality being uncommitted/non-aligned to any other country or group of allies.

no-man's-land waste land between two opposing sets of trenches.

ops shortened form of "operations".

orderly room room set aside for company's official business.

parapet top of trench.

platoon part of company – about 50 men.

private lowest rank in the army.

propaganda biased or distorted information.

puttees strips of cloth wrapped around a soldier's legs above boots.

quartermaster sergeant responsible for issuing stores to a company of men.

recruit someone who has just joined the armed forces.

regiment a unit of soldiers enlisted from a particular locality or for a specialized purpose (usually two or more battalions).

requisition to purchase compulsorily.

respirator gas mask.

reveille bugle call for soldiers to wake in the morning.

runner a foot messenger, in army.

sap a covered trench or tunnel dug towards enemy lines.

sapper private in the Royal Engineers.

shrapnel fragments of an exploded shell.

sniper marksman with a rifle.

subaltern commissioned rank below that of captain.

take posts to sight and range a field gun.

Taube type of German plane.

undress uniform uniform for everyday wear or for messy jobs.

Verey lights flares shot from special pistols to light up the ground at night.

waddi dry valley in desert.

Date List

1914

28 June	Assassination of Archduke Franz Ferdinand at Sarajevo.
1 August	Germany declares war on Russia.
3 August	Germany declares war on France and invades Belgium.
4 August	Britain declares war on Germany.
9 August	BEF lands in France.
23 August	BEF fights battle of Mons but is forced to retreat.
5-12 September	French troops check German advance in the battle of the Marne.
6 October	British Indian Army expeditionary force sent to Mesopotamia.
30 October-24 November	First battle of Ypres. German advance is halted in Belgium.
1 November	Admiral Cradock defeated by von Spee at Coronel, Chile.
5 November	Britain declares war on Turkey.
1 December	ANZACs arrive in Egypt to defend Suez Canal.
8 December	Admiral Sturdee destroys von Spee's ships off the Falkland Islands.

1915

9 January	First German airship raid on Britain.
24 January	Admiral Beatty wins battle of Dogger Bank.
10-13 March	Battle of Neuve Chappelle. British launch massive counter-attack against German line which fails.
17 April	Hill 60 near Ypres is mined and blown up by British.
22 April-25 May	Massive counter-attack by Germans retakes the Hill and pushes British back. Germans use chlorine gas for first time. Second Battle of Ypres: Britain holds on to Ypres.
25 April	Allied forces land at Gallipoli.
7 May	German submarine sinks Cunard liner *Lusitania*. Many American lives are lost.
23 May	Italy joins Allies by declaring war on Austro-Hungary.

6 September	Bulgaria joins war as Germany's ally.
25 September-8 October	Battle of Loos – new British offensive fails.
3-5 October	British and French troops land at Salonika to defend Greece against Bulgaria.
19 December	Haig succeeds French as British Commander in Chief. Allies start to withdraw from Gallipoli.

1916

9 January	Allied withdrawal from Gallipoli completed.
21 February	The French suffer a serious defeat at the Battle of Verdun.
29 April	Surrender of the British garrison at Kut in Mesopotamia.
24 May	Conscription begins in Britain.
31 May-1 June	Beginning of the Arab revolt against the Turks.
1 July-18 November	The Battle of the Somme.
15 September	First use of tanks, at the Somme, by the British.
7 December	Lloyd George becomes Prime Minister.

1917

11 March	British troops occupy Baghdad.
6 April	USA declares war on Germany.
9 April-4 May	Battle of Arras. Canadian troops take Vimy Ridge.
7 June	British troops take Messines Ridge and drive Germans back from the Ypres Salient.
31 July-10 November	3rd Battle of Ypres (Passchendaele). 5 miles of ground won at a cost of 400,000 British dead.
20 November-3 December	Battle of Cambrai. British launch surprise attack with 380 tanks but fail to follow up their early successes.
9 December	General Allenby captures Jerusalem.

1918

3 March	Russia leaves the war after signing the Treaty of Brest-Litovsk with Germany.

21 March-5 April German offensive on the Western Front drives 40 miles behind Allied lines.

14 April Marshal Foch becomes Commander in Chief of Allied forces in Europe.

15 July-7 August Battle of the Marne ends in German retreat.

31 October Turkey signs armistice with Allies.

11 November Germany signs Armistice.

1919

28 June Treaty of Versailles signed.

Places to Visit

For all aspects of life in the armed services at the time of the First World War, visit the _Imperial War Museum_, Lambeth Road, London SE1 6HZ (Tel. 01-735 8922)

For specialized collections of army vehicles and weapons dating from the First World War to the present, visit:

National Army Museum, Royal Hospital Road, London SE3 4HT (Tel. 01-730 0717)

Royal Artillery Regimental Museum, Royal Military Academy, Academy Road, Woolwich, London SE18 (Tel. 01-856 5533)

The Tank Museum (HQ Royal Armoured Corps and Royal Tank Regiment), Bovington Camp, near Wool, Dorset (Tel. 0929 462721)

For collections of aircraft, visit:

Duxford Airfield, Cambridgeshire CB2 4QR (on A505 Royston-Newmarket Road, by Junction 10 on M11)

The Fleet Air Arm Museum, Yeovilton, Somerset (traces history of Fleet Air Arm from its origins as the R.N.A.S.) Tel. Ilchester (0935) 840565

The Royal Air Force Museum, Hendon NW9 5LL (a comprehensive collection of WWI aircraft) Tel. 01-205 2266 (Nearest underground: Colindale on the Northern line)

The Shuttleworth Collection, Old Warden Aerodrome, Old Warden, Bedfordshire (vintage aircraft and army vehicles. Flying days in the summer) Tel. 076-727 288

For museums of naval history, visit:

The National Maritime Museum, Romney Road, Greenwich, London S.E.10 (Tel. 01-858 4422)

The Royal Naval Museum, H.M. Naval Base, Portsmouth Dockyard (Tel. 0705 733060)

The Submarine Museum, Walpole Road, Gosport, Hants (Tel. 0705 588035)

Lawrence of Arabia is mentioned in the text and readers may wish to get further information about his life or visit his cottage at Clouds Hill, near Wareham, Dorset.

Book List

Books for schools
Primary and middle
Gilchrist, Cherry, *Finding out about Life in Britain in World War I* (Batsford, 1986)

Hoare, Robert, *World War One* (Macdonald, History of the Modern World Series, 1974)

Martin, Christopher, *The War Poets – Brooke, Owen, Rosenberg, Sassoon* (Wayland, In Profile Series, 1983)

Morrison, Dorothy, *The Great War* (Oliver and Boyd, Exploring History Series, 1981)

Peachment, Brian, *Ready to Die*, a biography of Edith Cavell (Arnold Wheaton, Faith in Action Series, 1979)

Secondary
Hobley, L.F., *The First World War* (Blackie, 1971)

Huggett, R., *Growing Up in the First World War* (Batsford, 1985)

Liddle, Peter, *World War One* (Longman, 1977)

Longman Resource Unit, *The Great War*, a pack of 12 booklets (Longman)

Tames, R., *Living through History: The Great War* (Batsford, 1984)

Woodget, Dudley, *World War One, a Sketchmap History* (Longman, 1976)

Source Materials Suitable for School Project Work
Holt, Tonie and Valmie, *Till the Boys Come Home, Picture Postcards of the First World War* (Macdonald and Janes, 1977)

Imperial War Museum, *Trench Warfare* and *Women in Wartime* (Document Pack Series), facsimile documents and explanatory text; *The Western Front* (Photopack Series), dramatic black and white photos; *First World War Posters*, with captions and brief text. (All available from The Education Department, Imperial War Museum, Lambeth Road, London, SE1)

Moynihan, Michael, ed., *A Place Called Armageddon. Letters from the First World War* (David and Charles, 1973)

Simkin, John, *Contemporary Accounts of the First World War* (Tressell Publications, available from 139 Garden Avenue, Brighton, E. Sussex)

Staffordshire County Council Education Dept., *In Flanders Fields – a collection of accounts of life on the Western Front for School use* (Staffs County Council, 1979)

Tapert, Annette, *Despatches from the Heart, an anthology of letters from the Front* (Hamish Hamilton, 1984)

Vansittart, Peter, ed., *Voices from the Great War*, (Jonathan Cape, 1981)

For Older Readers
Allison, William and Fairey, John, *Monocled Mutineer* (Quartet Books, 1978)

Babington, Anthony, *For the Sake of Example – capital courts martial 1916-1920* (Leo Cooper, 1983)

Brayborn, Gail, *Women Workers in the First World War* (Croom Helm, 1981)

Brittain, Vera, *Testament of Youth* (Virago, 1978)

Brown, Malcolm and Seaton, Shirley, *The Christmas Truce* (Leo Cooper, 1984)

Campbell, Christopher, *Aces and Aircraft of World War One* (Blandford Press, 1981)

Coppard, George, *With a Machine Gun to Cambrai* (Imperial War Museum: Jane's, 1980)

Dixon, T.B., *The Enemy Fought Splendidly, a diary of the Battle of the Falklands, 1914-1915* (Blandford Press, 1983)

Ellis, John, *Eye Deep in Hell* (Croom Helm, 1976)

Graves, Robert, *Goodbye to All That* (Penguin, 1960)

Hough, Richard, *The Great War at Sea* (Oxford University Press, 1983)

Macdonald, Lyn, *They Called it Passchendaele* (Michael Joseph, 1978)

Macdonald, Lyn, *Somme* (Michael Joseph, 1983)

Middlebrook, Martin, *The First Day on the Somme* (Fontana, 1975)

Parsons, I.M., *Men Who March Away, Poetry of the First World War* (Chatto and Windus, 1968)

Winter, Denis, *First of the Few, Fighter Pilots of the First World War* (Allen Lane, 1982)

Index